I0467822

THE ACCESS CODE
HOW TO UNLOCK YOUR SUCCESS

J DEMETRIUS BARKER

CONTENTS

FOREWORD

INTRODUCTION

PIN 1   1
HOW TO OVERCOME OBSTACLES

PIN 2   4
HOW TO FIND SUPPORT

PIN 3   6
HOW TO DEVELOP A DREAM OR GOAL

PIN 4   9
HOW TO LOCATE YOUR PASSION

PIN 5   12
HOW TO NEVER QUIT

PIN 6   16
HOW TO SECURE FUNDING

PIN 7   19
HOW TO START A BUSINESS WITH NO MONEY

PIN 8   21
**HOW TO INFILTRATE ENVIRONMENTS THAT SEEM
OFF LIMITS**

PIN 9   23
**HOW TO SUSTAIN YOUR SUCCESS AND CREATE
A LEGACY**

ACKNOWLEDGMENTS   28

NEW RELEASES   30

SUCCESS WORKSHEET   31

FOREWORD

A seed.

It is placed in the ground; when it is properly watched and watered, it will grow.

It is placed in the ground; when it is properly watched and watered, it will grow. J Demetrius is one of those seeds. He started from being planted in a dream. The seed kept growing as he applied himself to different jobs and activities. The seed kept growing to the point that he became a motivated young entrepreneur!!

In this new and inspiring book, J Demetrius will show you the steps on how to make it and survive the weeds and storms that could hinder the seeds of success. I have watched him over the years and I know that he has the zeal and enthusiasm to help and guide you through whatever problem you may encounter in your journey to success and achievement.

It's always a blessing to be a blessing to someone else and this book will bless you to unleash all the seeds of greatness that is in you. seeds of greatness that is in you.

Dr. Jimmie A. Ellis, D.D

INTRODUCTION

Before we get started allow me to introduce myself. My name is J Demetrius and I am a twenty-six-year-old serial entrepreneur. I currently co-own a three-story salon and Spa in Philadelphia, I am the editor-in-chief for Hair Follicles magazine, which I also own, and I am the founder and the Head Leader (CEO) of Advise Me, Inc. a coaching and marketing firm. I am the former co-founder and chancellor of Urban Entrepreneurs, an organization that focused on equipping youth with the tools and connections to start their own business or enter the career field of their choice.

I have extensive customer service and sales experience. I served for seven years as a customer service representative for the city of Philadelphia. I have held positions in sales and administration and as a Business Strategist with small and large corporations. At Jim Smith Jr. International I strategized marketing and branding campaigns to increase exposure and revenue. When I worked for the Philadelphia 76ers Inside Sales I outsold my colleagues by 30% every night. I currently teach sales professionals and entrepreneurs how to brand, market, and sell their products and or services.

So those are a few of my credentials. Here is the flip side...I am not a college graduate. I didn't say I didn't go, I said that I didn't graduate. I study business law with a concentration in contracts at Pierce College. I have also completed coursework in Organizational Leadership at Ohio Christian University.

Now that we got that out of the way let's talk about how a twenty-six-year-old has managed to accomplish all of this without a college degree and money.

My reason for writing this book is to give you the access code to success. I am going to show you how to set goals and get things done. In this reading you will learn the following pin codes:

1. How to Overcome Obstacles

2. How to Find Support

3. How to Develop a Dream or Goal

4. How to Locate Your Passion

5. How to Never Quit6. How to Get Funding

7. How to Build a Business with No Money

8. How to Infiltrate Environments That Seem Off Limits

9. How to Sustain Your Success and Create a Legacy

Pin 1
How To Overcome Obstacles

What is an obstacle? My definition of an obstacle is something that wants to discover who you are. Here is a bonus for you, let's just call it Pin 10. I promise you will have a different mindset, perspective, focus, and drive after reading this book. Hopefully, you are up for the challenge. If so, let me hear you say, DEAL!

OKAY. Obstacles do two things. Number one, they challenge you. Two, they arise to find out who you are. Many of us go through life and claim to be one thing but when faced with a challenge we fail to show up.

As a young man growing up in the inner city of Philadelphia, I often experienced gang-related activity and bullying. In our society today bullying is ubiquitous. There is cyber bullying, political bullying, religious bullying, bullying in the workplace, and physical bullying.

When I was sixteen years old, I stood at five feet six inches and the bully was about six feet. Every time this individual saw me, he had something negative to say or found a way to taunt me. One day, on my way home, I rode past this guy and he threw a basketball into the back of my head. I stopped the bike grabbed the basketball, and flung it back at him. He dodged it, of course, but it didn't stop there.

He walked across the street and punched me in the face. I decided that this obstacle was no longer going to stand in the way of my peace. I put my hands up and the fight started. Now, what he did not know was that I had taken several martial arts classes. There we were, hands up, ready to fight. I was livid. He looked as if he was about to eat me alive. He threw another punch, this time I hit him with a roundhouse kick directly in the rib cage. He grabbed his ribs and threw another punch. Each time he threw a punch I threw a kick. I didn't try to block the punches because my focus was not on stopping the punches but on eliminating the puncher. Five roundhouse kicks later he put his hands down and walked away.

That day I learned that whatever you claim to be will be tested. Secondly, I learned that bullies and obstacles need to know that you are no pushover. Whatever the current obstacle is that you are facing requires your immediate attention. Don't waste time worrying about what happens if you get hit, focus on reacting to what's in front of you and eliminating the puncher. Eliminate the source of the obstacle rather than dwelling on the danger the obstacle poses.
Now, you may not be getting bullied in the sense of physical harm. You may be experiencing emotional or economical punches. I want to give you some steps to eliminate your puncher.

Step 1. Identify where the punch is coming from (why are you being punched?).

Step 2. Strategize how to eliminate the puncher.

Step 3. Be courageous enough to face the fight head-on.

For someone reading this, your puncher may be in debt, denied by the bank, or in an old relationship. No matter who or what the puncher is it can be eliminated.

Identification, strategy, and courage, now that you are aware that this obstacle has entered your life and based on what I told you above, you can now show up for the fight. You may get punched in the process. If you are diligent like I was and keep kicking eventually the puncher will retreat, FOREVER.

Pin 2
How To Find Support

Support is a common factor of complacency. People who allow the lack of support to stop them from achieving their dreams/goals never get the chance to grow. Failure is a gift and until individuals see it as a gift, they will never be successful.

Okay, how to find the right support? You don't! If you are lucky, you may have two or three people who truly support you but, even those individuals will not support you one hundred percent. Either they will support you by giving money, or they may promote you or attend an event. Either way, you don't find support, you build it.

Please write this on your forehead, "There is no individual on this planet capable of helping, supporting, or even loving me the correct way." You have to build the support you need. Great leaders understand that for them to accomplish their goals they have to build a team.

I have friends who are business owners, doctors, lawyers, and religious leaders. A common problem among them is finding the right help. To see such gifted individuals, remain stifled because of what someone else will not do baffles me. So, being the effective coach that I am, my first question is: Do you have money to pay for the help? Most

4

likely the answer is no. If that is the case, my advice is, to build them. When I say this, I am always met with confusion. Build them? Yes, build them. There is no one on this earth currently equipped to deal with you. Your teammates will have to learn who you are, what you like and dislike, how you work under pressure, how you react when you're hurt, or how you react when frustrated and angry.

If you need support in any capacity, I suggest that you find willing individuals and train them. Here is a little tip for married and single people...your mate has NO idea how to handle or even love you but, guess who does...you. It is best if you teach them (through a passive strategy) how to do so. This will remove the frustration brought on by expecting someone to be something that they are not. Have you ever been to build a bear or cold stone? Both companies have adopted this theory of allowing individuals to build what they desire. This limits waste and promotes happiness. If you need help invest the time and train your help how to help you.

Pin 3
Developing a Dream or Goal

First, let me outline the stages of developing a dream or goal.

Phase 1. Write what you see (write it down).

I deliver a keynote entitled "Execute on Vision" and what that means is, to build what you envision and nothing less. You need clarity on what you desire to accomplish and why you want to accomplish it.

Phase 2. You need to identify the obstacles that MAY stand in your way (write them down).

Phase 3. You need to develop a strategy to overcome those obstacles (write it down).

Phase 4. You need impenetrable focus.

Phase 5. You need to be consistent in the strategy

When I was 16 years old and a sophomore at Roxborough high school in Philadelphia I met a guy named Raheem in the mock trial club. Raheem and I started an organization called Urban Entrepreneurs. We wanted to start a business where we could help our peers start their businesses. So, we sat down with my mentor, Corey K.

He helped us brainstorm a business plan and marketing strategy. After we had locked down all of the preliminaries, we approached our school with the idea of starting this club. Due to our reputation with the faculty, we were able to get the club approved. That same week, we held our first open house for members. During our first open house, thirty students joined and it grew to about sixty members.

Our first event was an empowerment breakfast; we had no way to fund this event. We needed a venue that would rent to teenagers (we didn't tell them that we were), tickets, flyers, and a reason for people to come. The first stop we made was Docucare to have the tickets designed, the cost for design and printing was $50. We didn't have the money but we were determined to get this done.

We walked two miles down to Quiznos on Broad Street and asked to speak with the manager. We showed him the flyer and a sample ticket with the cost written on the back of it. We explained the purpose of the event and why it was important for him to help us. He went into the office and came out with a check for the total amount. We were so shocked that he just gave us the money, being young, black and in a city where crime is prevalent, we couldn't believe it. We thanked him and walked back to the print shop and had the tickets printed that same day. We sold the tickets to family and friends for fifty dollars. Maybe about thirty people attended the event but we had a mission and a strategy, and we were focused.

Here we were, two high school teenagers with no business experience and barely any life experience, raising money and hosting empowerment events. I won't give you the entire story, just know that we opened a cafe in the school and we employed all of our members. They were paid in course credits and got out-of-class free passes from time to time. We had a mission, strategy, and guts. We went on to help two individuals start businesses and others secure internships in their desired industries. What is your mission? Is your mission compelling enough to provoke action from yourself and others? Your mission has to drive you first and then everyone else.

Here's a bonus: only tell your goals to qualified individuals. Here is how you qualify them, evaluate their life and see how much risk they take. Secondly, listen to their conversation. Is it a billboard or wallet-size talk? Individuals who have the wrong speech have the wrong mindset.

On your journey to success, your perspective will be your number one asset. You will always need a good (informed) and fresh (evolved) perspective to be a success.

Pin 4
How To Locate Your Passion

This is a very commonly used word in our society so let's substitute the word passion for the word obsession. If I were to ask you what is your passion you would probably say golfing, singing, cooking, helping people, and things like that. But when I ask you what is your OBSESSION immediately your mind goes to one or two things.

Okay so my passion is leading people, I have always wanted to be the leader. But it's not my obsession. My obsession is helping people win. It took me some time to figure this out, here is how I did it:

Since I was a child, I never liked people being left out, I always felt like it was my duty to make the underdog feel included or liked. I remember there was a kid named Corey and he was a little chubby and soft-spoken. As you can probably imagine that's a recipe for bully-me pie.

Now, the kid that got punched at sixteen years old is not the kid in elementary school. This kid is the leader of his gang. We called ourselves the ducks, corny right? We called ourselves that because one of the members (Anthony) was slew footed. So, we all walked like that, lol. As I write this, I am CTHU (cracking the hell up). One day we were at recess and the gang and I was practicing our walk across the schoolyard I saw a group of people picking on Corey. Immediately I start walking over toward them. Of course, the "ducklings" followed.

When we got there, I pushed the crowd away and he was crying with snot running down his nose. He said thank you and I told him to come and get me if they messed with him again. I think they were taunting him about his uniform or something. Nevertheless, I just always seem to hate people being picked on. I remember watching movies like "never back down" where the main character was picked on or counted out for whatever reason and I noticed that I would just go bonkers when they beat the bully up or overcame their obstacles.

So, I learned that I love seeing people win. I love to see people beat the odds. This single discovery has driven my success to this day, seeing people take the shitty hand they've been dealt and create a masterpiece with it.

So, why did I say you would locate your passion? Because you will! To help you get past what we call your passion which is nothing more than hobbies. We need to identify what makes you a fanatic. What are you super persuaded to do? Here is the key to your obsession, when you pinpoint your obsession, will host everything you need to keep going. In the book Be Obsessed or Be Average super salesman Grant Cardone talks about his obsession with success. Grant explains how he embraced his obsession and pulled himself out of the gutter.

" The obsessed embrace the fact that they –and only they – are responsible for their success." @GrantCardone

Your obsession holds enough inspiration, motivation, money, and fulfillment to sustain your desire to achieve. It becomes your "manna" from heaven. You may do your passion for free, and after a while, it will bore you, but your obsession will pick you up and make you keep going. Make a list of your passions and make another list of the things that you are obsessed with. Here is my list:

Passions:
- Music (house)
- Golf
- Cooking
- Leading
- Business

Obsessions:
- Helping People Win
- Making Money

Make your list...

How To Never Quit

The first way to never quit is to identify your obsessions and hone in on them...and NO, your obsession is not something that you would or could do all day for free. Your obsession is that thing that keeps surfacing from your childhood. You can profit from passion but you can thrive on obsession. I have a question for you...Are you a quitter? Yes, or NO?

Prove it! Make a list of everything you've accomplished in the last six months...

MAKE YOUR LIST

1.
2.
3.
4.
5.
6.
7.

Okay, after making your list how many of the things listed were intentionally accomplished? Meaning, these items were already on your goal list. Or did you just write down the good things that you did in the past six months? Remember success happens on purpose. You will never stumble upon success; you have to make some preparations and you have to take immediate action.

I was once a product salesman for an MLM (multi-level marketing) company. My greatest success in MLM was when I was a member of The M.A.D Team. This was an organization of like-minded, big-dreaming, hardworking, and dedicated individuals.

I was twenty-two years old at the time, I had already been involved in several other MLM companies before but this one was different. I had the opportunity to meet billionaire John Wadsworth and two millionaires, Dr. Art Lee and Mrs. Valencia Pamphile. I was introduced to the company by my uncle James. The company's concept was familiar since I had already sold health products before and the money looked even better. So, I paid my sign-up fee and I immediately got to work. My hard work and ADHD-like demeanor created a buzz about me. A week later the team was having an appreciation event for members who outproduced the rest.

While at this celebration I had the chance to meet the millionaires and see firsthand how they loved to give back. There were several prizes given out that night. One prize, in particular, was a paid cruise to the Bahamas. Here I was, twenty-two years old and broke, but I knew that I was in the right place. Unfortunately, because I had just joined the team I did not qualify for the cruise. Luckily the millionaires over-purchased rooms. They held a dance contest and of course, I jumped up and claimed my spot on the floor.

This was the longest thirty minutes of my life but, I was determined to get on that ship. First, I had never been out of the country and I had a passport (prepared) secondly, it was an opportunity to get close to the sharks (millionaires), and thirdly what else did I have to lose (perspective).

I and all the other unqualified people prepared for battle. Some danced and quit within two minutes, others ran out of dance moves but, I held in there until the end and I lost. I lost the contest. I was up against three women and in a room full of men...what else is to be expected. But luckily one of the ladies was stupid enough to take a flat-screen TV instead of the free cruise. And the sharks gave it to me, DOPE! I was ecstatic.

Why did I win? Firstly, I took the risk. Secondly, I knew this was my only shot at getting a millionaire mentor. My advice tip for you is when you want to gain access to an environment, you have to create favor.

Here is how I was able to get a millionaire mentor. I was taught by my mother to always show your appreciation when someone is kind to you. So, I went to the Swarovski Jewelry store and I purchased the best pair of earrings and cuff links that I could afford. Once I was on the ship, the first thing I did after unpacking was stopped at the concierge desk and ask if I could have the items delivered. I told the concierge how I wanted the gifts delivered and what time to deliver them...you have to be strategic! That same day during our team meeting I received the opportunity to speak to the entire team about my experience with the team. See ladies and gents you have to be consistent and persistent in order to obtain what you want. I knew that for me to develop into the person that I wanted to be I needed guidance from someone who knew how to get me there. I only shared this story with you because I want you to see how the smallest of goals require persistence. As you develop your success strategy remember, success is not guaranteed it's optional.

Pin 6
How To Get Funding

Step 1. Identify how much funding you need. Have you done the math?

Step 2. Make a list of traditional fundraising methods. Step 3. Make a list of your fundraising ideas.

Step 4. Identify which fundraiser can be accomplished with donations.

Here's an example:

Let's say I want to start a non-profit organization and I need to file for my 501c3, get marketing materials, and have some operating capital to get started.

- Funding Needed: $5,000
- Fundraiser: Donations
- Sources: social media (personal network, like-minded individuals and their network). Let's say I have a combined following of 6,000 people between all my social media platforms.
- Petition: "I am asking for each of my followers to support this amazing cause. We are asking for a donation of only $2. If each willing person who is dedicated to making a difference donates just $2, we will reach our goal."

- Duration: Make this a thirty-day campaign and within ten days you should have over $3,000.

You're Welcome!

Step 5. Reach out to your network to support the cause, NOT YOU. Many times, people think that others will support them but that's not one hundred percent true. People will get on board to support a cause before they will lend you a penny.

Step 6. Take action. You need to have a series of events back to back until you reach your goal.

LISTEN, one event is not enough even if you reach your goal within the first ten minutes. You need to have daily and weekly activities. Host at least seven events within a span of two weeks. Aggressive, I know, but you have to be aggressive to achieve your goals. Passiveness and happenstance will only get you a mouth full of regrets and a head full of grey hairs.

What is your funding strategy? Crowdfunding bootstrapping, hustling, angel investors…write it down. Identify a list of clients or persons willing to invest and or PRE-pay for services so you can use those funds to scale.

Use the next page to jot down some funding ideas.

Pin 7
How To Build A Business With No Money

YOU CAN'T! There is no such thing as building a business with no money, even if you use someone else's money. My first business fortunately was not Urban Entrepreneurs. It was a candy stand that I had outside of my house. In 2004 my momma lost her job and things got rough but we were resourceful so we made it work. I remember one day she handed me an access card. I was perplexed. I looked at the card and back at her like, "What am I supposed to do with this?"

I had just completed my freshman year of high school and I wasn't old enough to get my working papers so my momma said, "You need to do something." I asked if I could open a store in front of the house and she said yes. So, I took that lime green and yellow card to the grocery store and I purchased three gallons of Hawaii Punch juice, a case of chips, ten dollars of candy, sodas, and cake mix. I was already known for baking cakes in the neighborhood so I used that as my marketing strategy to drive traffic to the store. I had tremendous success. I made enough money to repurchase what I needed and enough to pay myself. Technically, I did not have any money, but I had an ACCESS card. Now I have a three-story salon and day spa, a coaching firm, and a magazine. It only takes a mission and a drive to get things done. I guarantee that the reason you are having so much trouble executing is that your mission is not compelling. When your mission is compelling, it moves YOU first. You may not have the money but **SOMEBODY** has the money. ASK!

Whom can you ask? Who has the Money? Who likes you? Who favors you?

Name: _____

Name: _____

Name: _____

Pin 8
How To Infiltrate Environments That Seem Off Limits

Remember the story of the millionaire mentor and how I was able to gain access? That's a big factor in accessing guarded environments. Gaining access to "members only" environments will take a risk. Also, you will need confidence. Lastly, you must recognize your moment.

If you pay close attention, there is a common theme throughout this reading, and that is focus. I may not plainly state it but it's implied. You have to be focused to achieve your goals. Had I been concerned with how I was going to get to Miami and get back home, I wouldn't have had the opportunity to sit in the millionaire's suite and ask him questions about business and his life. Here are the exact steps you need to take to gain access.

Step 1. Locate the ACCESS point

Step 2. Build your reputation and credibility by creating a buzz

Step 3. Get a gift ready

Step 4. Identify your moment to enter the environment

Step 5. Wait for the moment to SOW (not show) your appreciation

I promise no environment is off-limits to you. You must have a _____. If you do not have a Strategy, you will offend instead of flatter. Dr. Lee's and Mrs. Pamphile's exact words were, "We have never seen such class from anyone in this industry. Young man, you are going to go far." Strategy is the key to success. Without a strategy, you will cause more damage than progress.

Pin 9

How To Sustain Your Success And Create A Legacy

No business is worth investing in if it cannot be duplicated. Do you remember the advice I gave on support? Insert that same advice here, you must first have a strategy and secondly, you must build the help that you need to sustain your mission.

Building for legacy does not begin when you are about to retire, it starts the day you decided to have a career, attend college, start a business or start a family. Your plans need to be documented and established legally to ensure longevity. I advise all of my clients to "put their stake in the ground permanently."

I do not get involved in any business deal that does not allow immediate and long-term profitability. Not one or the other, I must have both.

For example:

If you are a graphic designer and someone asks you to design a t-shirt image and let's, say that your fee is $300 for design setup and a few corrections. If you know that the client has a large clientele or is business savvy, propose no

upfront cost to design (maybe $50) and ask for a $0.25 per t-shirt royalty throughout perpetuity.
Let's do the math:

$0.25 Your Fee x 2,000 t-shirts = $500 Royalty

Every person should focus on making their presence in the world permanent. Linear income vs. passive income, which one do you want? Every highly successful person has passive income. Oprah, Elvis, Grant Cardone, and Beyonce all have multiple streams of passive income. This is the type of income made from leveraging other people's efforts. This results in nice, thick, monthly, quarterly, and annual royalty checks.

The way you build a legacy is by identifying what you desire. Secondly, you need to develop a strategy to get there. Lastly, you need to execute continuously.

1. Where/What (desire)
2. How (strategy)
3. When (deadline and continuous action)

This is a sequence that should be repeated consistently to ensure long-term success. The following questions will help you formulate your legacy plan.

1. What do I want?

2. What do I not want?

3. Why do I want to keep this under my control?

4. Why should this business, concept, property, or insurance policy be kept?

5. How do I ensure that my plans will be carried out?

6. Who is the best candidate to carry the plan?

7. Is this sustainable for the next wave of trends and generations to come?

8. If I am not dead in twenty years (you never know), what would my business specialize in?

9. Do we as a company, family or organization need to change what we focus on today to own tomorrow?

10. What problems do I see arising in the next decade?

11. Do I have things in place to answer/solve the problems of the future?

12. Will this idea be in demand next year?

13. Do I have key member/employee insurance for my business?

14. Do I have a will?

15. Who am I willing to train?

16. When will I retire?

17. What infrastructure do we need to improve?

18. Who may be a hindrance in the future?

19. Who am I willing to tolerate?

20. Have I exhausted my potential?

Answer these questions and they will help you formulate your legacy plan. You need to get ahead of this today. I am certain you are aware of the ever-changing world we live in. Danger can live next door to you, hell, danger can be in the same bed with you. So be proactive and outline the strategy for your family, business, and estate. The key to achieving those dreams you have is to revisit them daily. Keep your goals in front of you and secure a system for success. A common thread between successful people, relationships, businesses, and ideas is systems. Duplication is only possible when there is a system in place. Many times, when I meet with new clients, their number one issue is lack of focus.

Systems eliminate focus problems. I advise anyone attempting to start a business, build a family, or pursue an education or career; to first develop a process to produce. Multi-millionaire Marcus Lemonis from CNBC's The Profit has a standard approach to investing in businesses. His approach is "people, product, and process." Marcus understands that without a process people have no direction and the product will be inconsistent. I am uncertain what your goals are, but if you do not establish a system, you will always miss the mark. Systems and processes ensure success and longevity. Revisit your plans and identify if you need to develop a system for sustainability in order to build a legacy.

Remember, life is what you make it. Your decisions will decide what happens to you and I hope that this reading has been informative, inspiring, humorous, and action-provoking. Remember, you can only become successful if you are willing to develop a strategy and take a risk in implementing that strategy. Follow the steps and advice outlined above and you will always have the access code to living a successful life. Please, I beg you to take time and carefully re-read the advice above. Complete the exercises and watch how your life radically changes in the next few months.

Your Coach, J Demetrius

Acknowledgments

Many individuals are not named that have been great sources of support. Thank you all and remember that I am constantly and forever rooting for you all to win.

Shirley Pickett

Dr. Jimmie A. Ellis III

Herb & Karen Holmes

Bill Raymond

B. L. & P. G. Garrison

Dr. George & Ella Taylor

Jim "Mr. Energy" Smith Jr.

Raheem Harvey

Corey Kirby

Dr. Art Lee

Mrs. Valencia Pamphile

Pastor Larry V. Daniels

Grant Cardone

For editing contact Jason Howard via email at JasonHoward3@yahoo.com

I WANT TO BE YOUR COACH!

We offer solutions in these key areas:

1. Business and Professional Coaching
2. Keynotes
3. Mastermind

How do you see it? This question can change your life forever. It's how you see a thing that determines if it gets the best of you or if you get the best of it. A mentor causes you to go farther faster. Choose to go farther by signing up for my mastermind group today.

Book J Today @ JDemetrius.com

MY ACCESS TO SUCCESS WORKSHEET

Below is a very crucial exercise to get you moving in the right direction IMMEDIATELY.

MY SUCCESS WORKSHEET

Let's do an exercise that I do with my coaching clients. In the spaces below identify your top two goals. The first goal should be a three-month goal. This goal should be engagement-focused. This is where you and your team should be in the field adding value and building relationships. Host and attend events that build momentum and perpetual social engagement… this will keep your pipeline full.

GOAL 1:

MY SUCCESS WORKSHEET

The second goal should be a six-month goal. This goal should be revenue focused. I know normally businesses focus on quarterly benchmarks; however, I found that it is best to break these goals down into a revolving systematic process. Now, you should always be providing value and closing deals. This goal should be specific to a mission or campaign. Maybe it's a global initiative, social cause, or internal customer retention plan. The three-month goal provides the traffic to fulfill this benchmark. Implementing this works as a strategy to lay out what is needed, what's missing, and how to prepare, and it acts as a clear path to achieve what must be done.

GOAL 2:

MY SUCCESS WORKSHEET

It is extremely important to eliminate all possible hindrances that you can foresee. One major factor that prohibits people from going after their dreams is what MIGHT happen. So, write down what MIGHT happen so that you may prepare for it and know how to respond IF something happens.

Write them down!

1.

2.

3.

4.

5.

A note from J...

Go after your dreams. They are achievable. You must have a clear vision. Find an example to model after, everything doesn't need to be original. YOU are already original so do something that's already been done just add YOU to it. It isn't easy building and starting over but you can win. Honestly, you've already won. Through many ups and downs, you've made it. Look back at those things you've conquered and see where the gold is. Don't allow the "small" things in your life to go unaccounted for. Remember they were once big things. You must have a strategy. Nothing in life works without strategy and systems. When you think you've run out of options, think again. Don't be an island, someone has traveled this way before. Even if they haven't, I am certain someone has traveled part of the way... find the other parts. Do you see what I am doing? I am making it very difficult for you to give up. You are so close. Get there! YOUR process IS the gold. Now, excavate it, purify it and showcase it to the world. I wrote this book in two days, inspired by Grant Cardone. Someone has traveled this way before. This book is a small snippet of my process but it is gold. Share your story, it's time to change lives!

"You may have to change how you get there but NEVER change getting there."

-J